I0486438

HALLOWEEN
COLORING BOOK

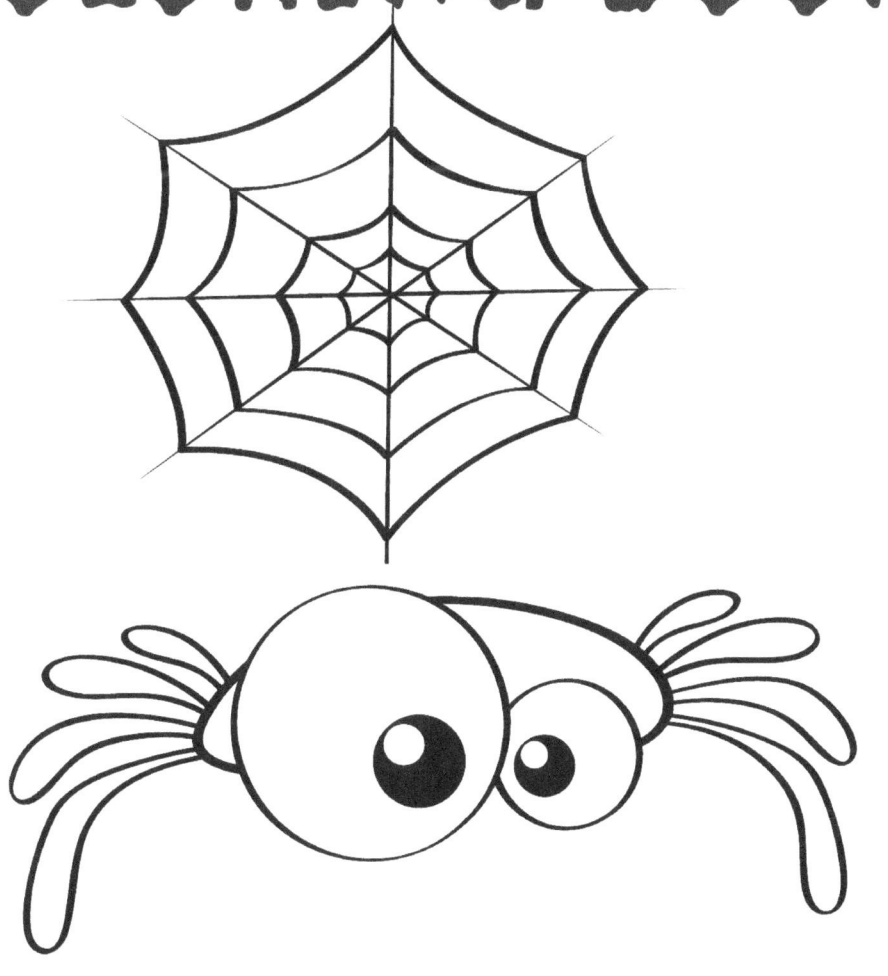

By L.R. Billy

Published by L.R. Billy in 2015
First edition: First printing
Illustrations and design © 2015 L.R. Billy

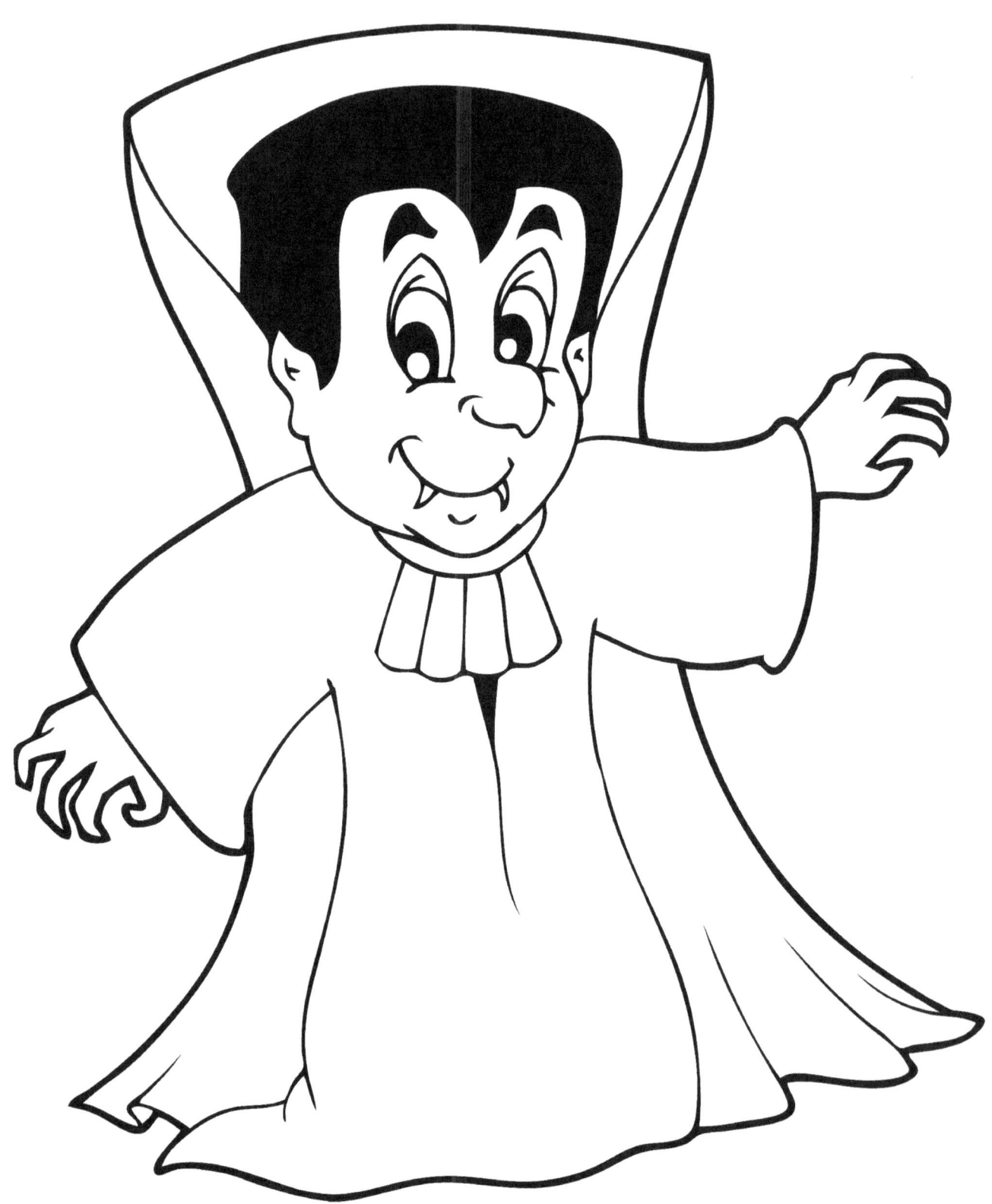

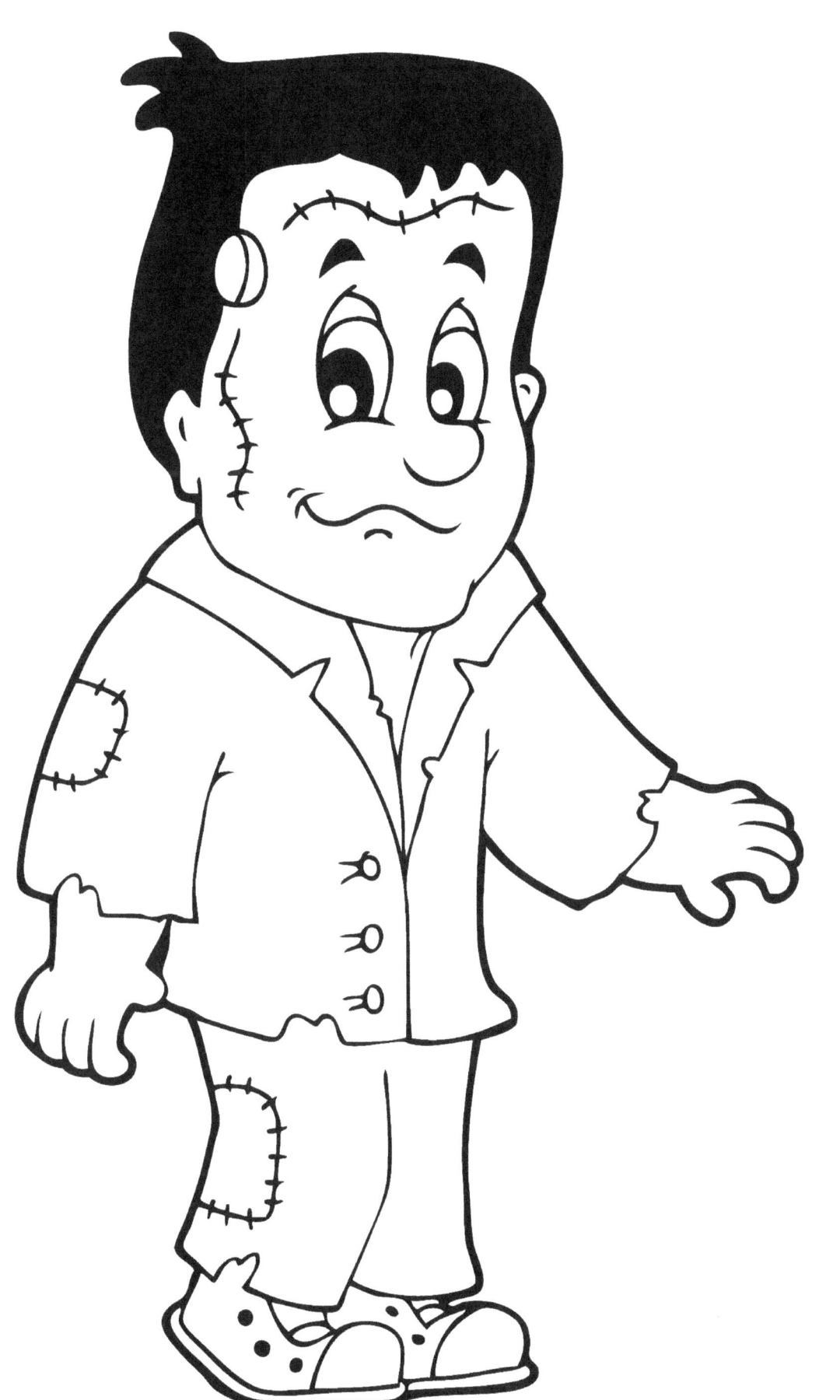

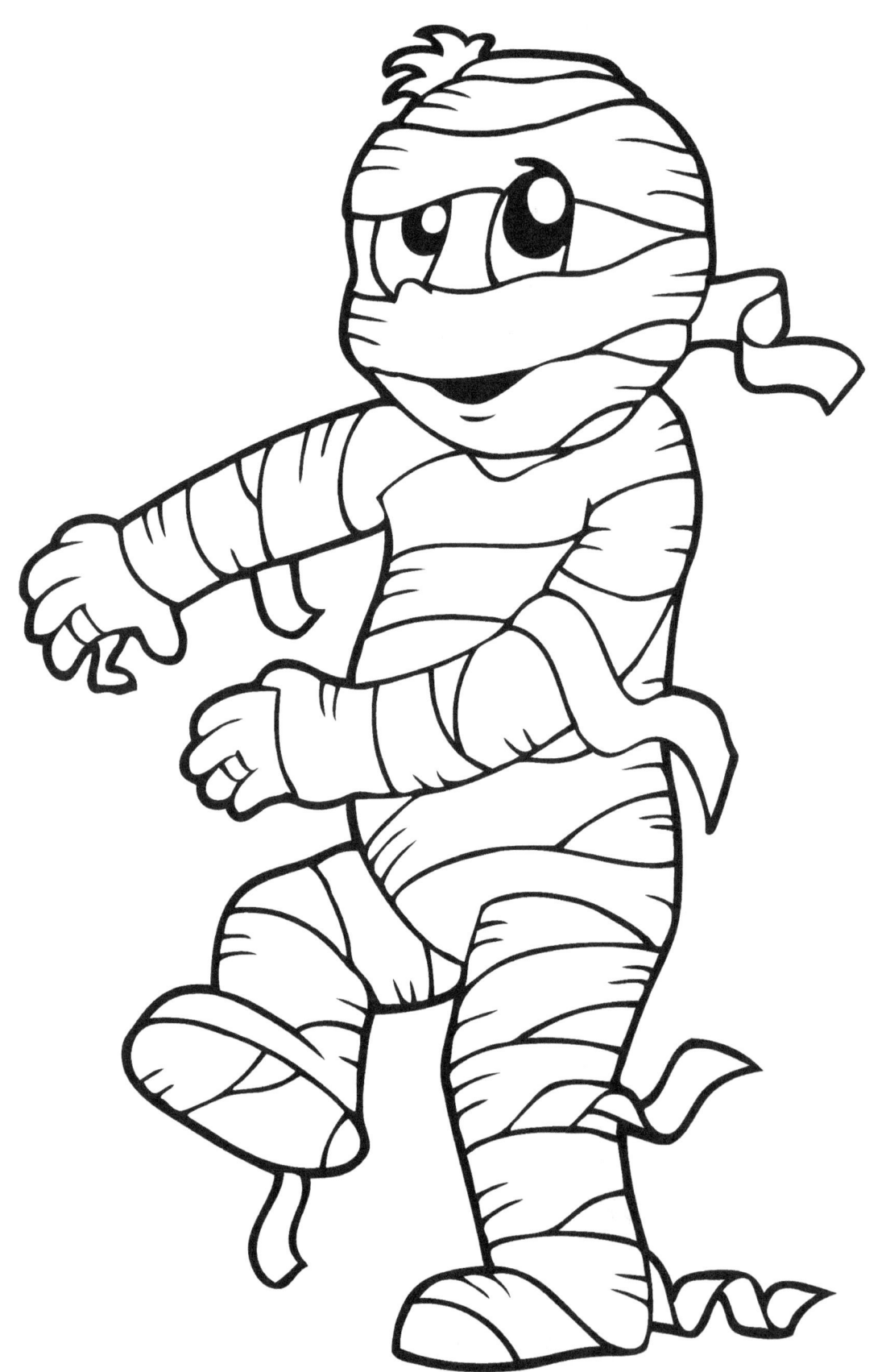

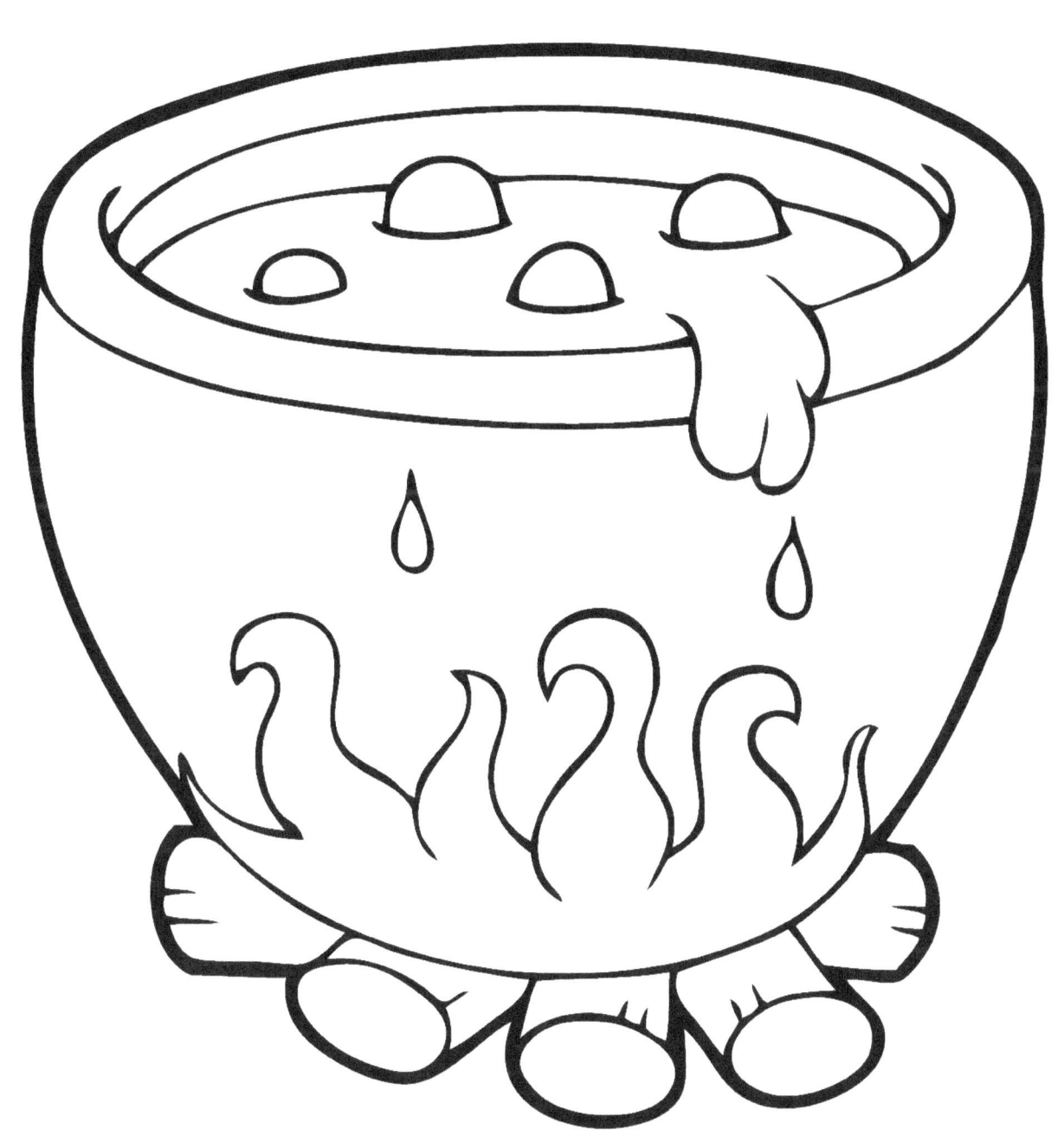

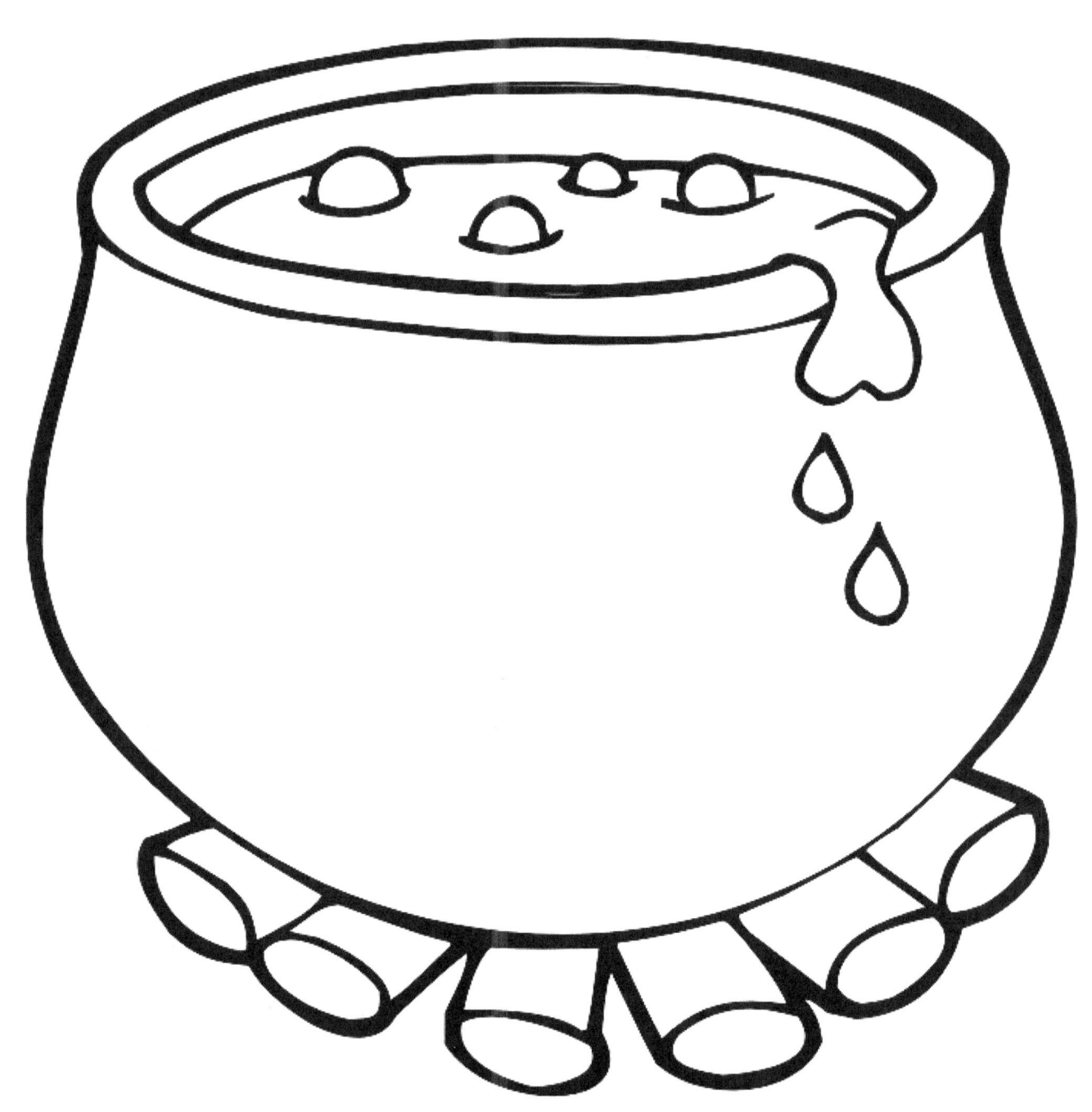

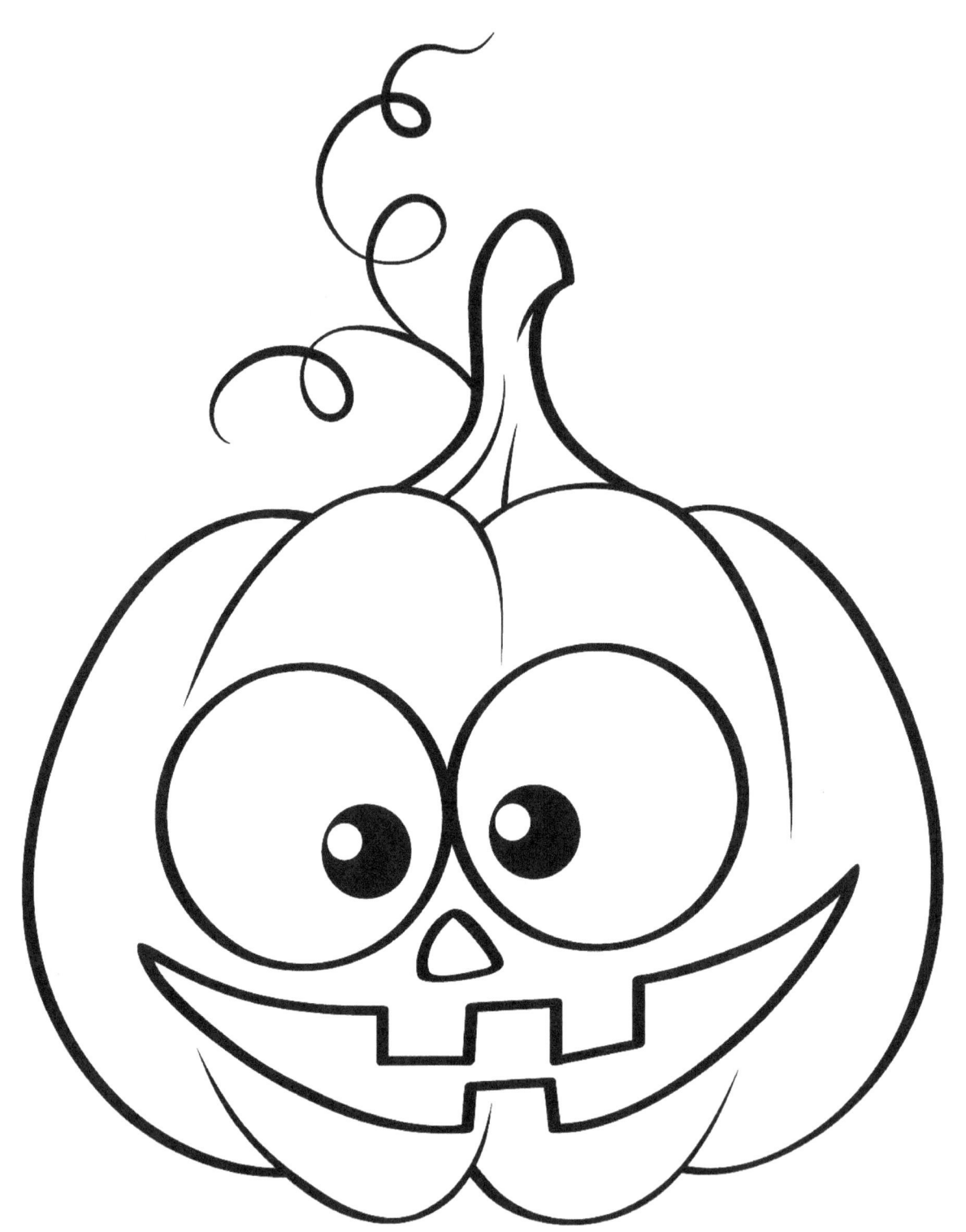

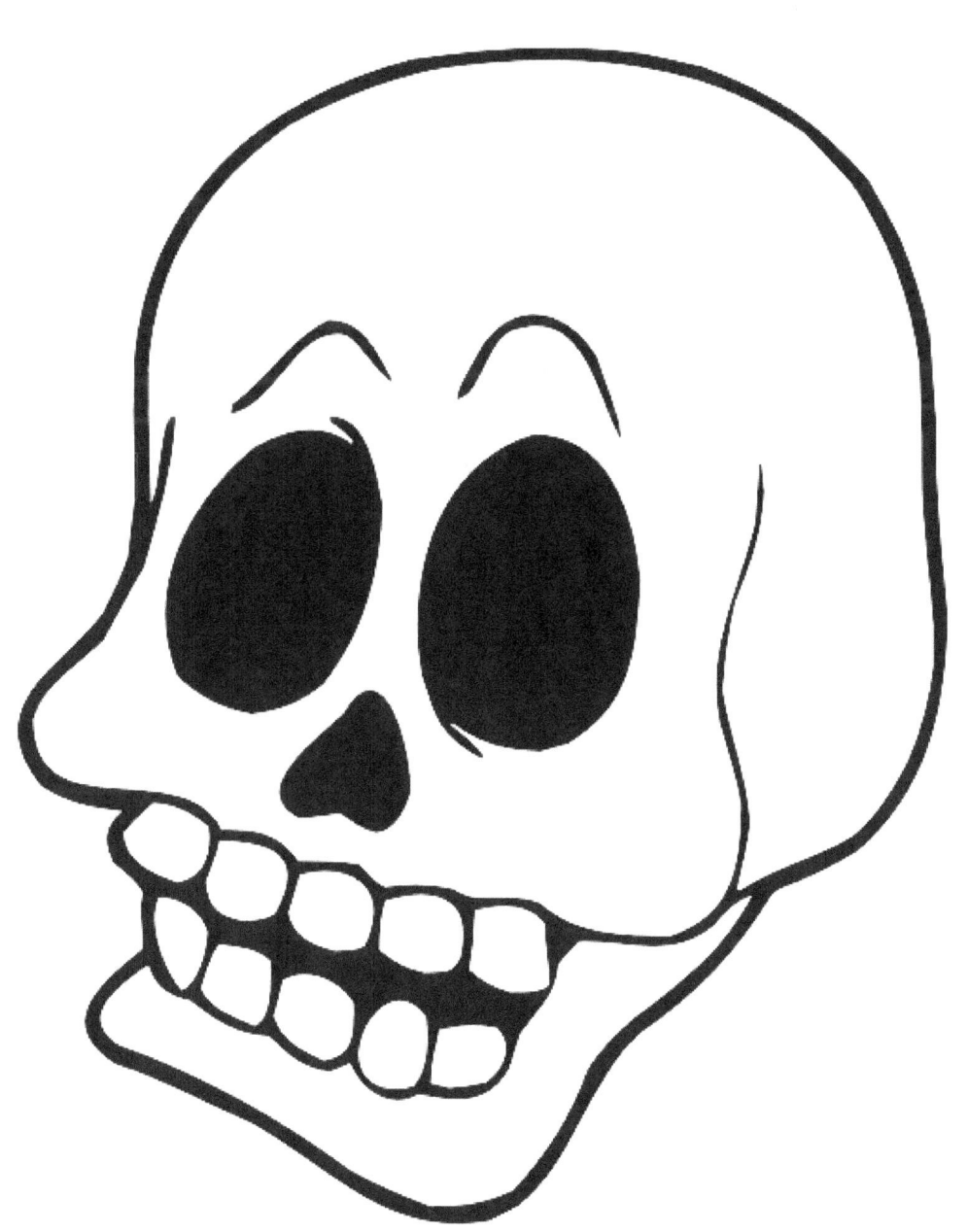

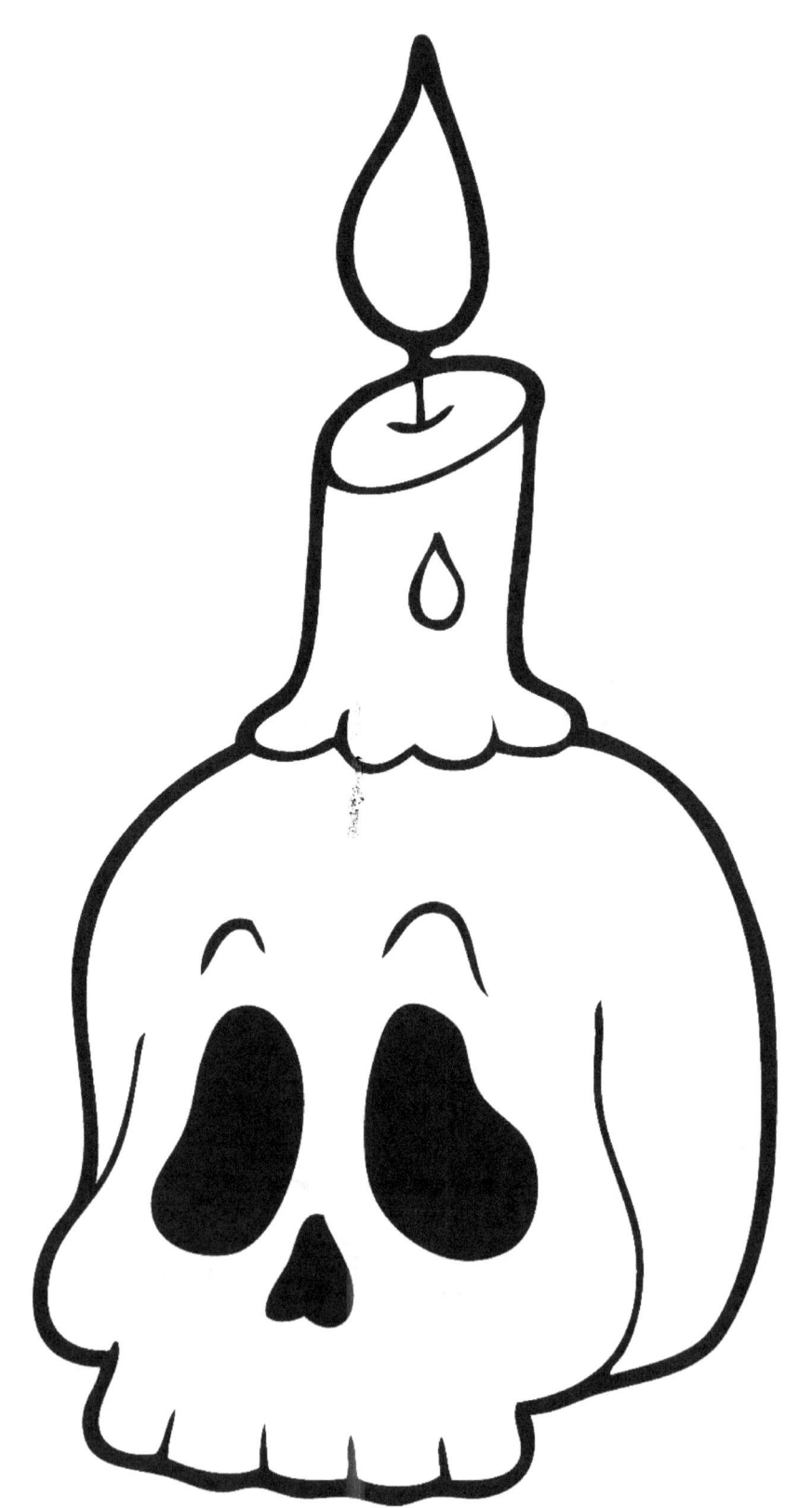

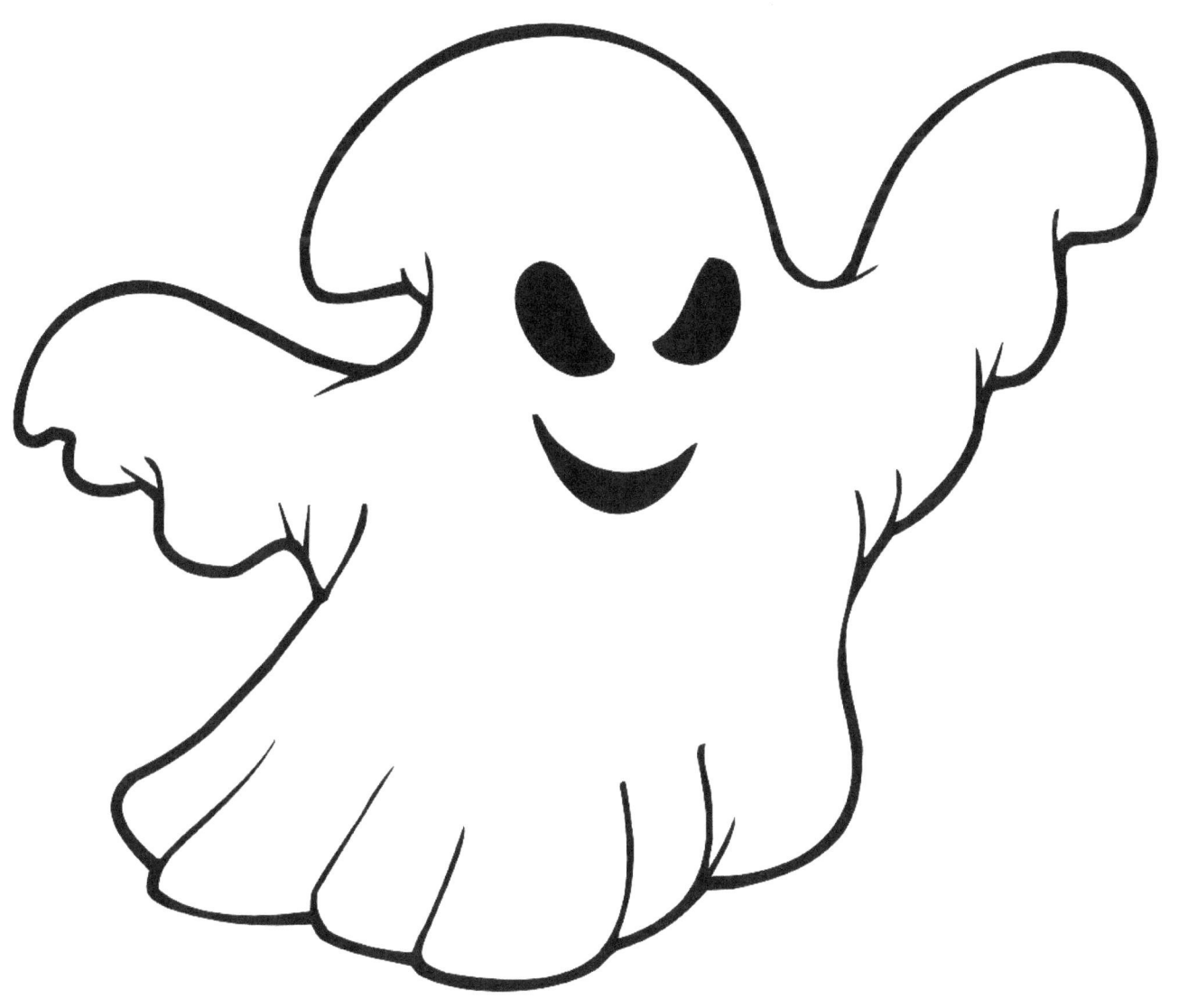

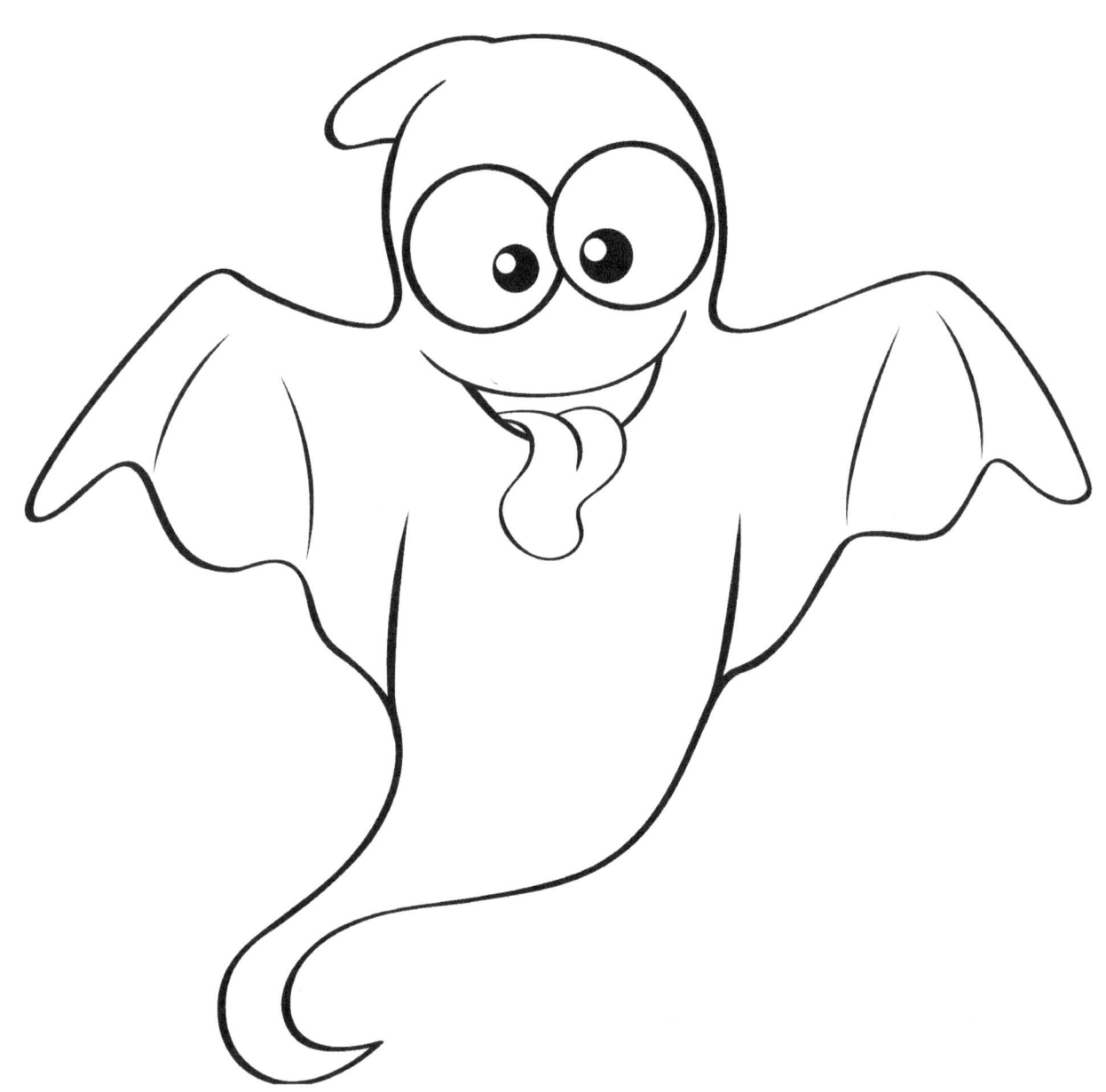

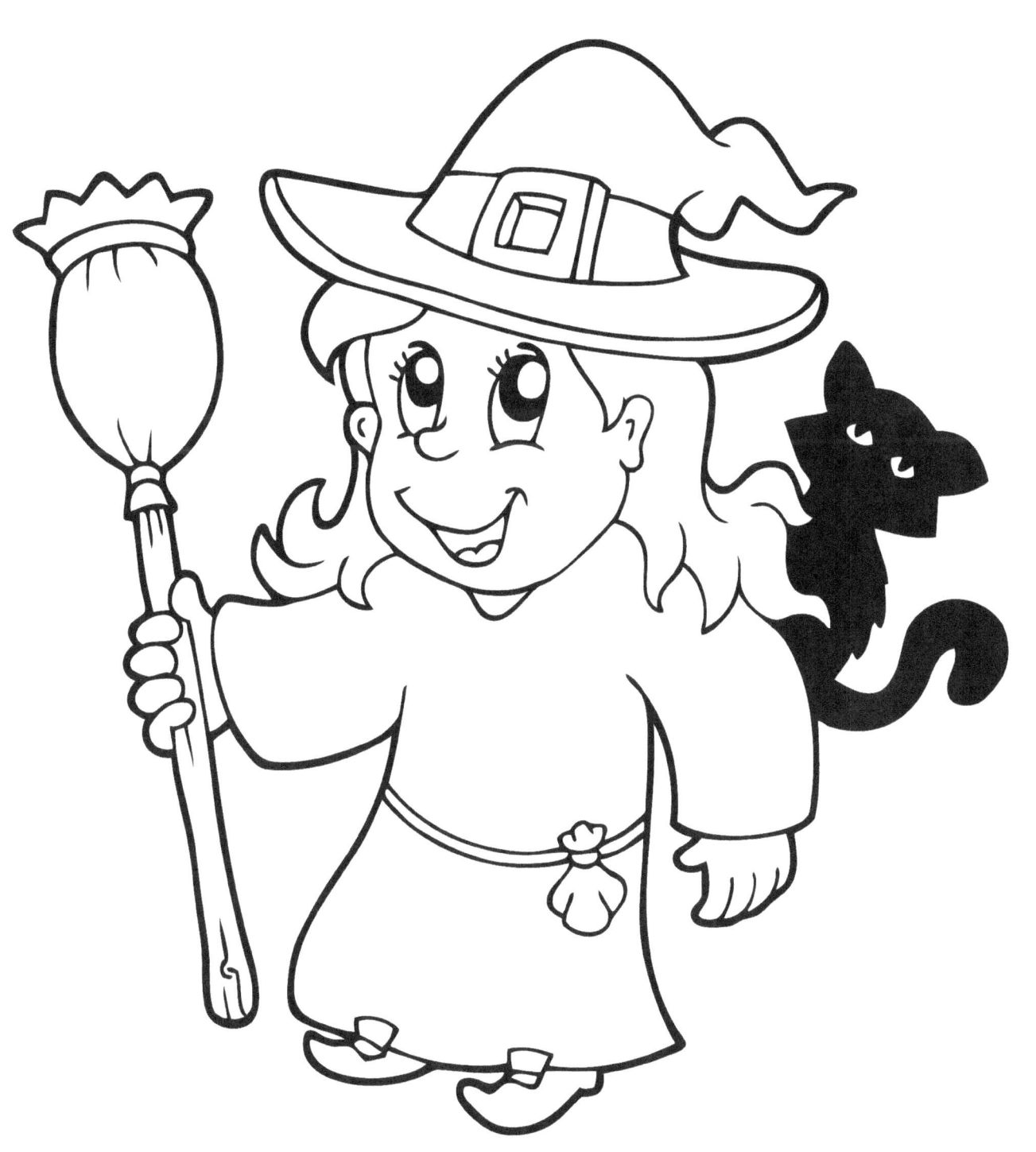

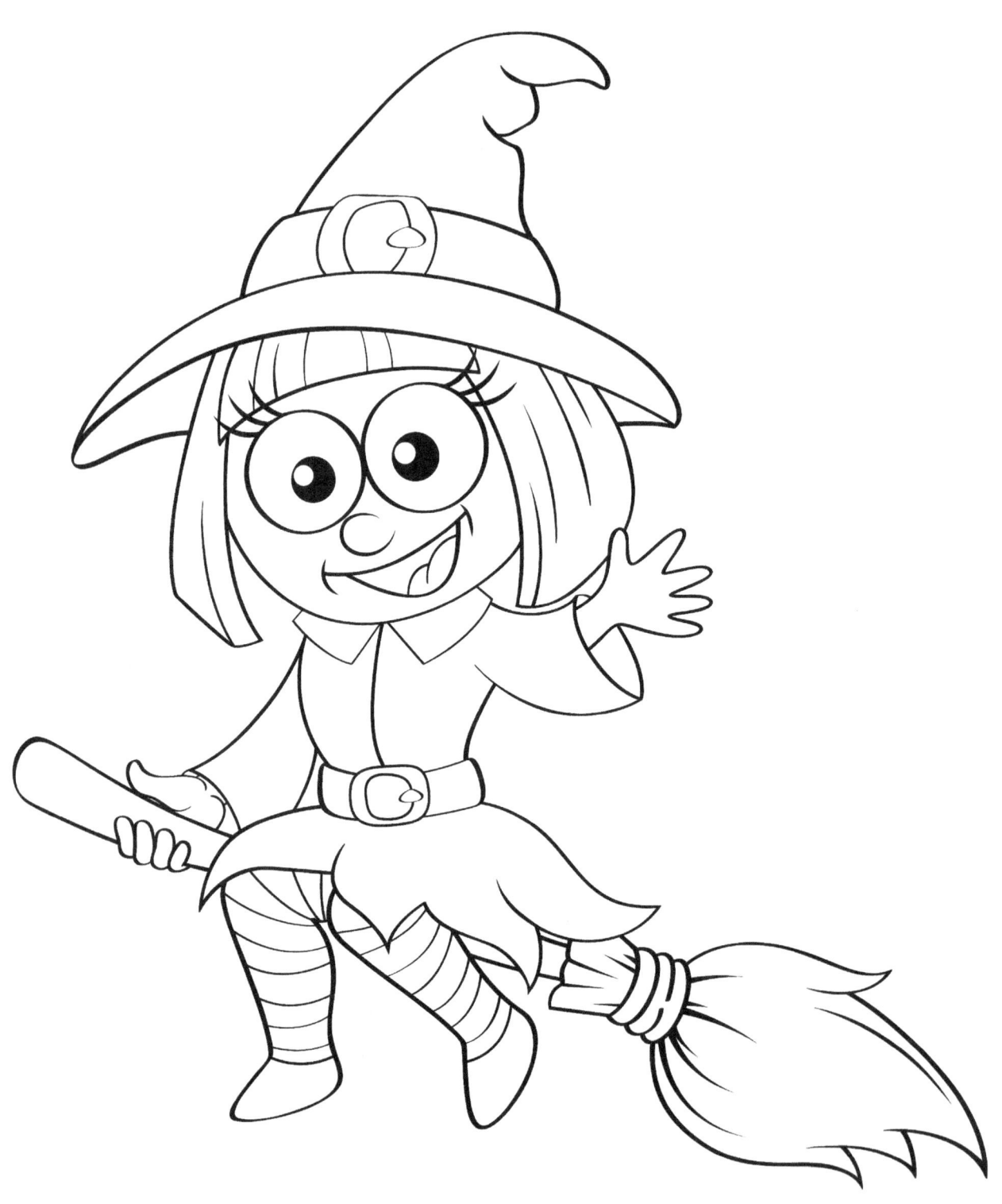

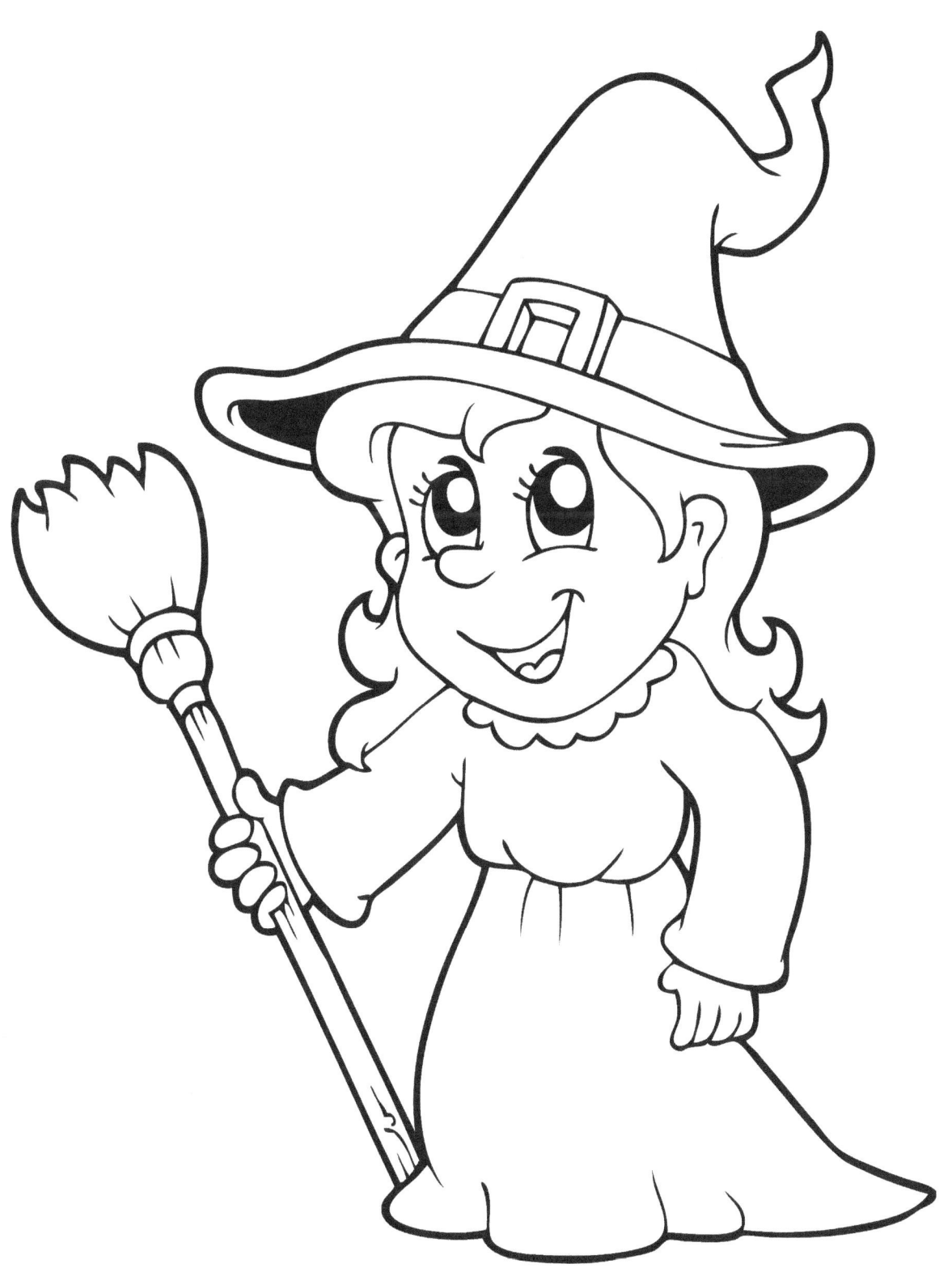

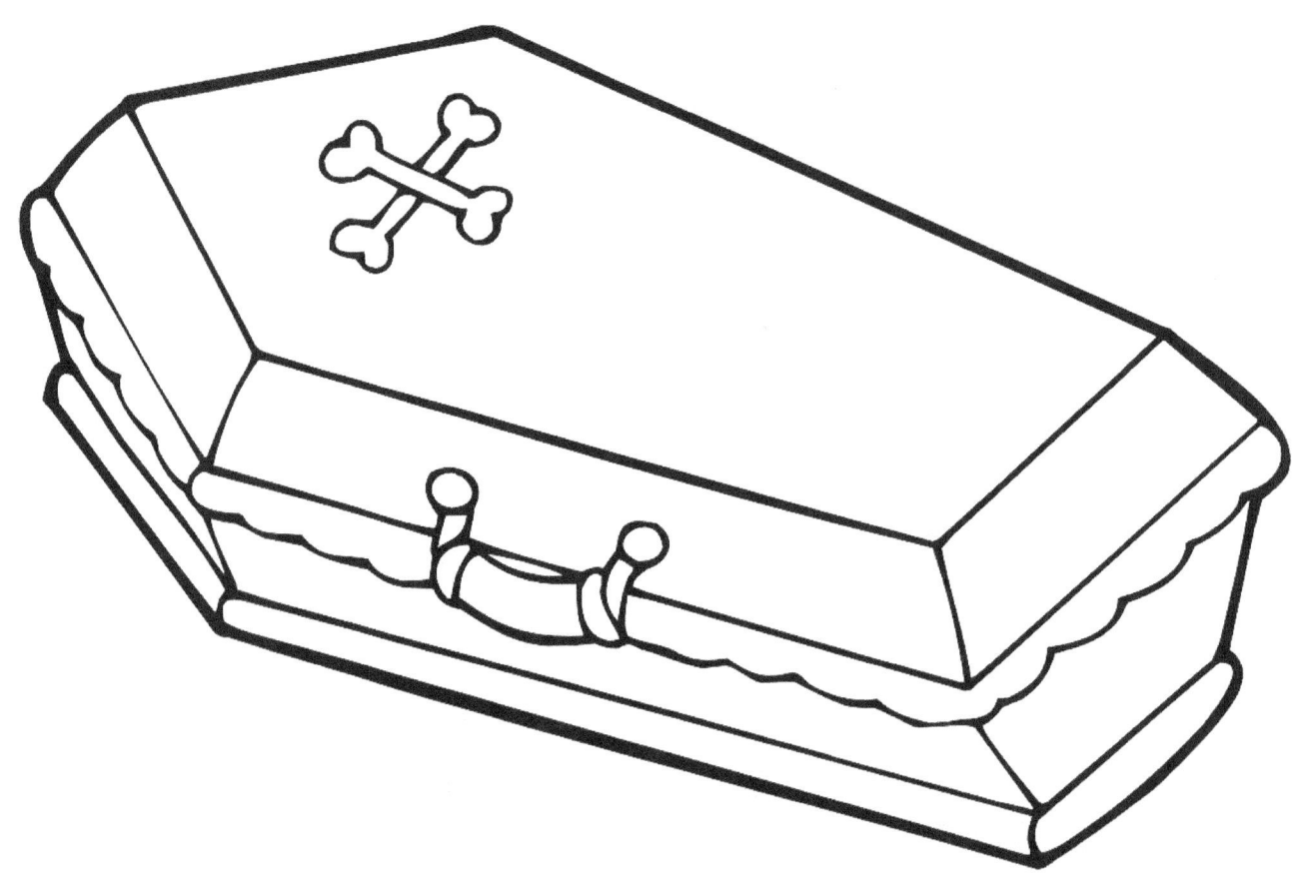

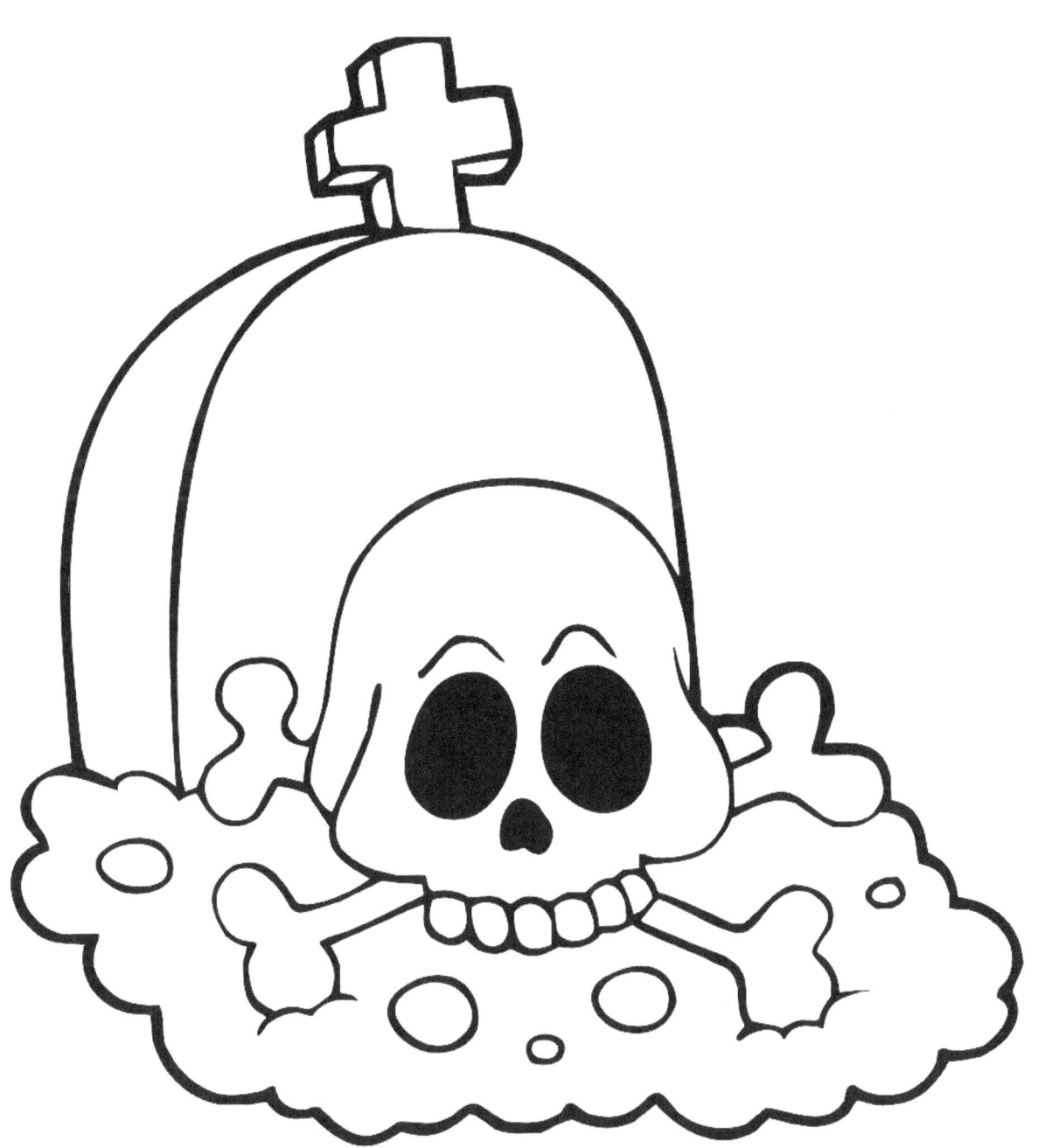

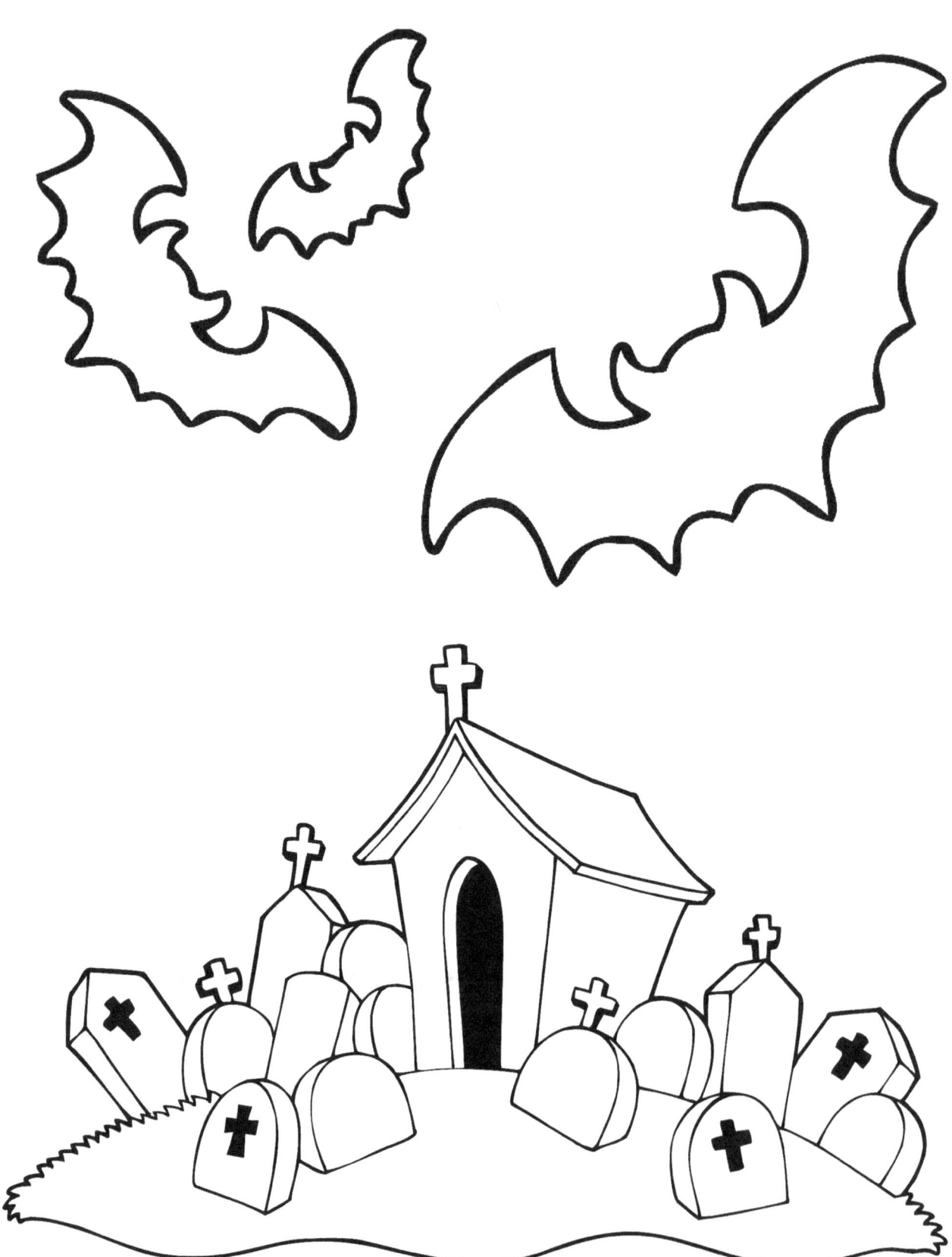

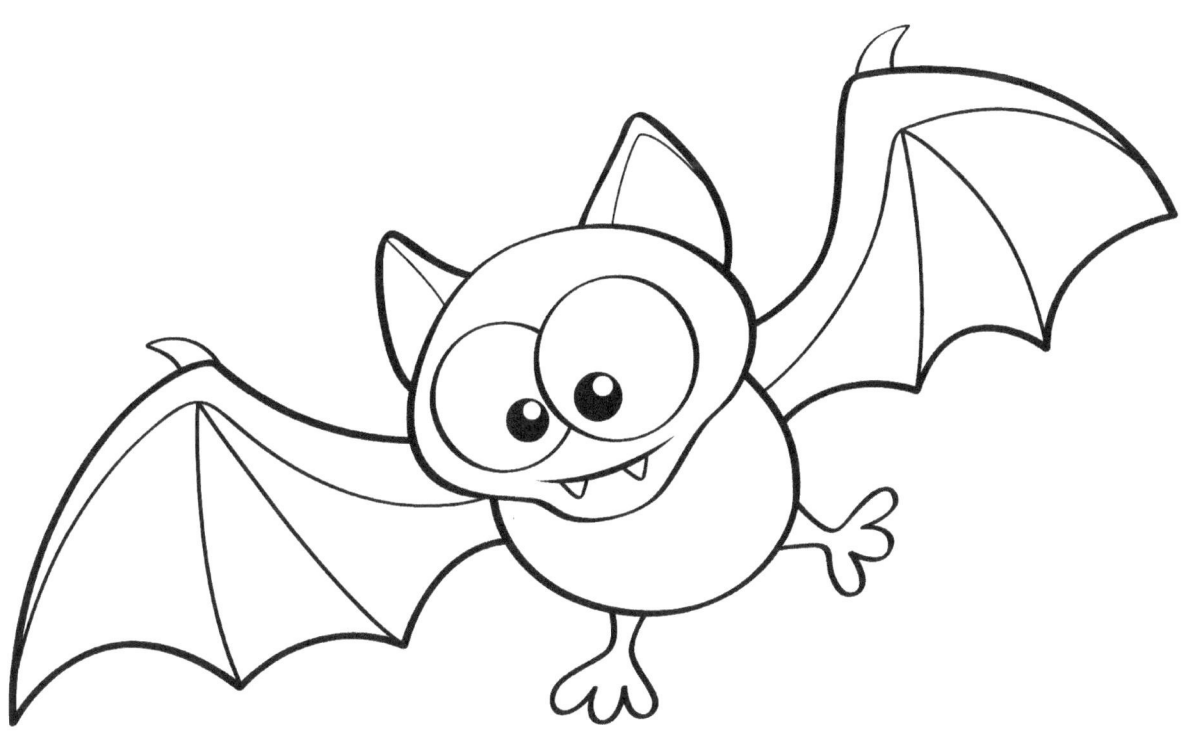

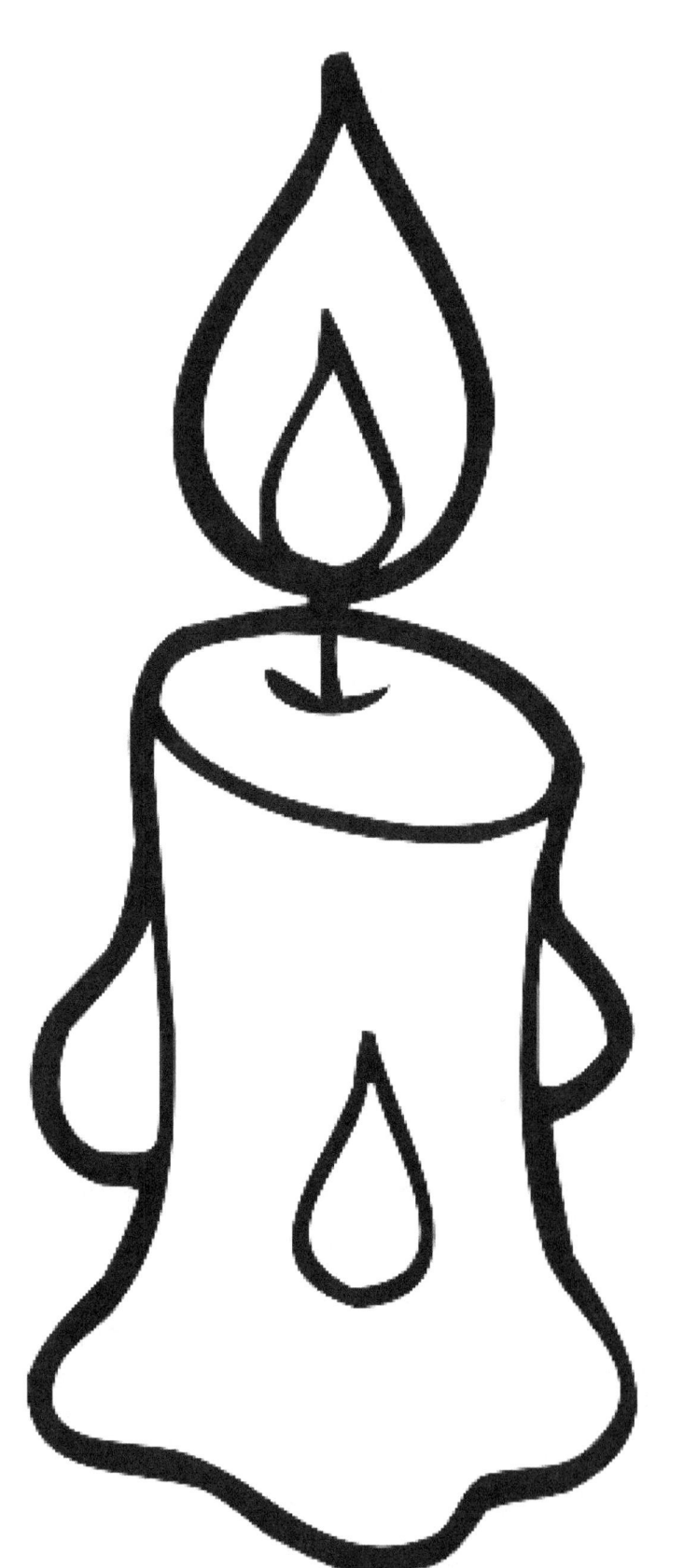

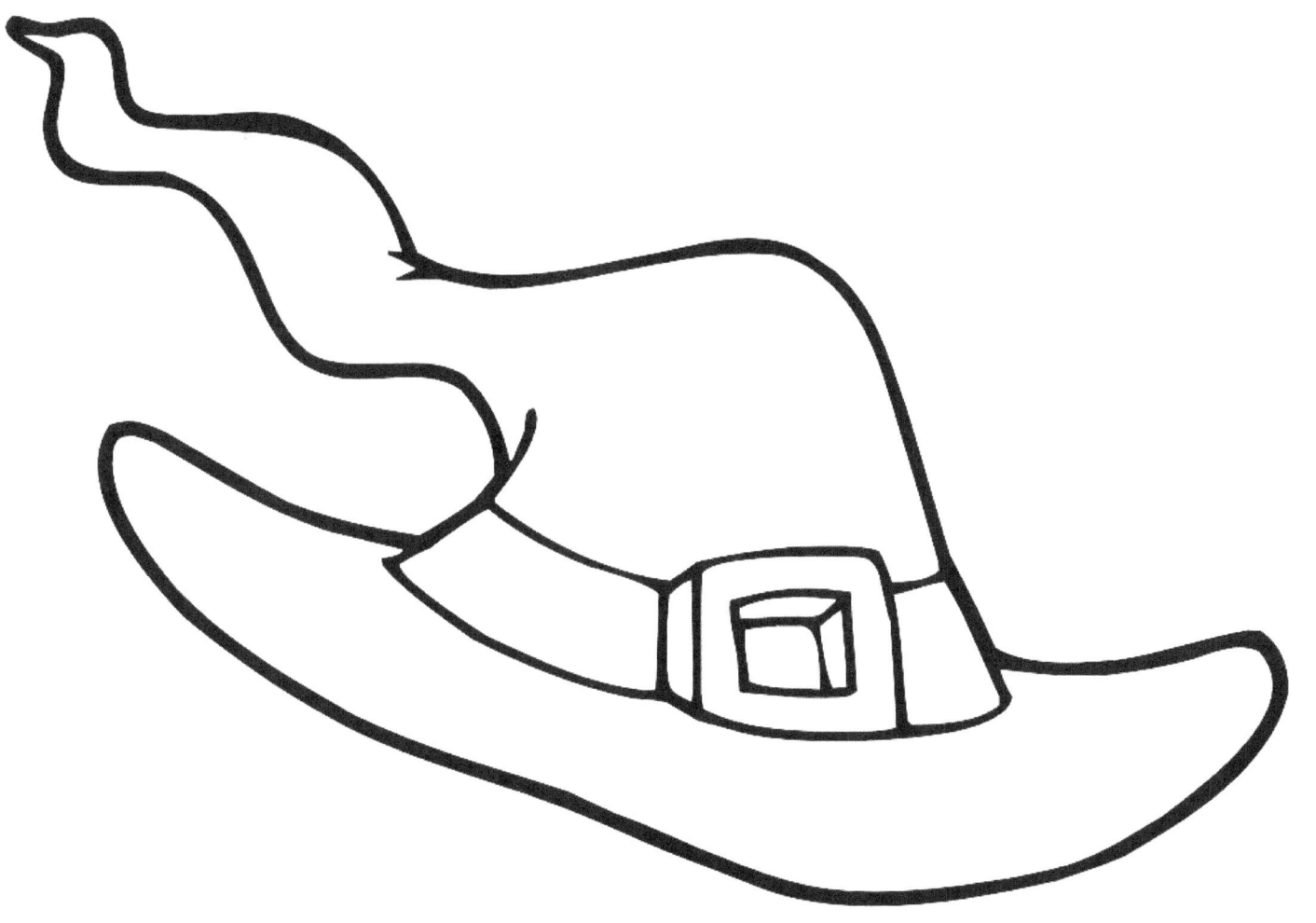

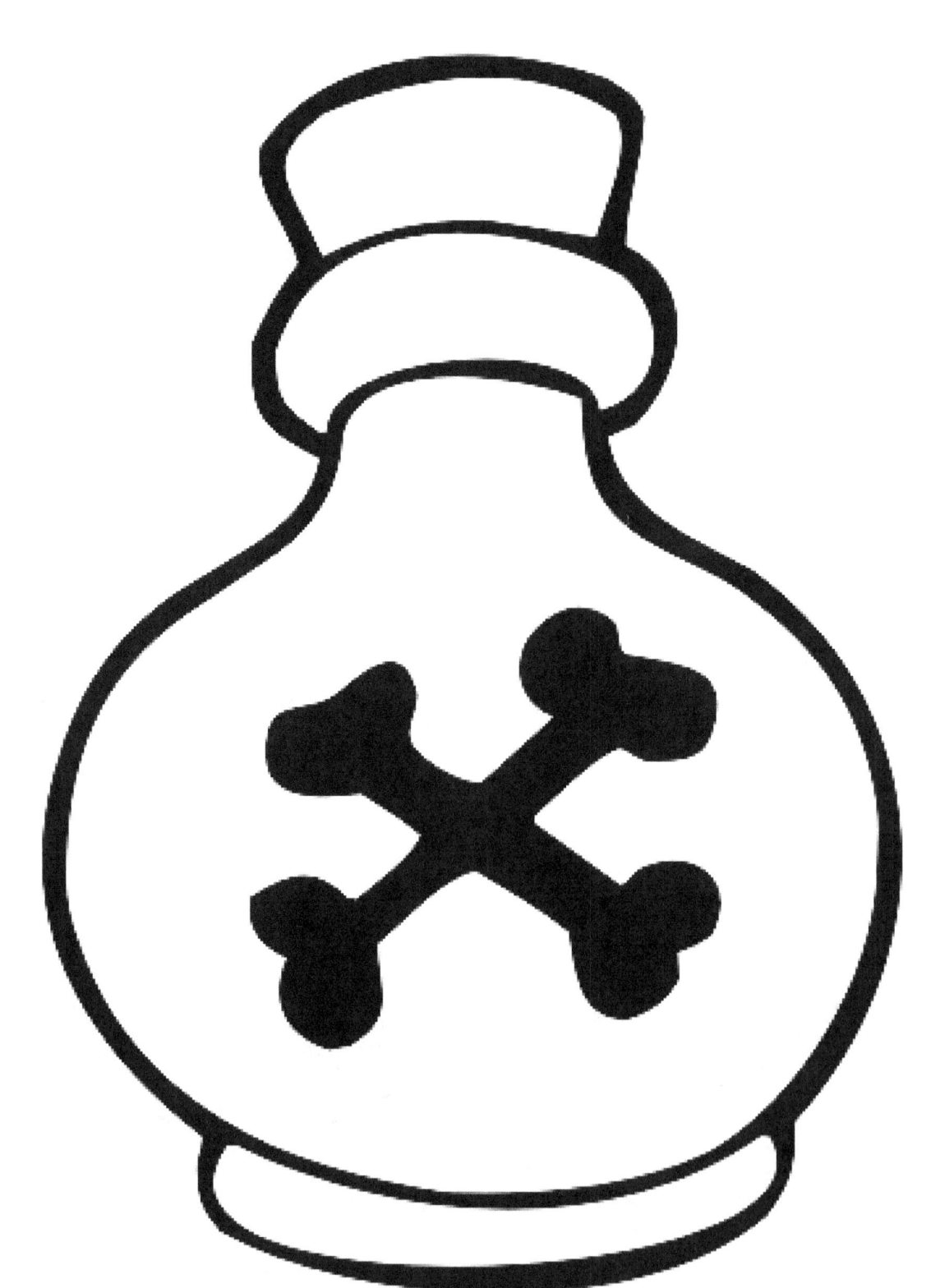

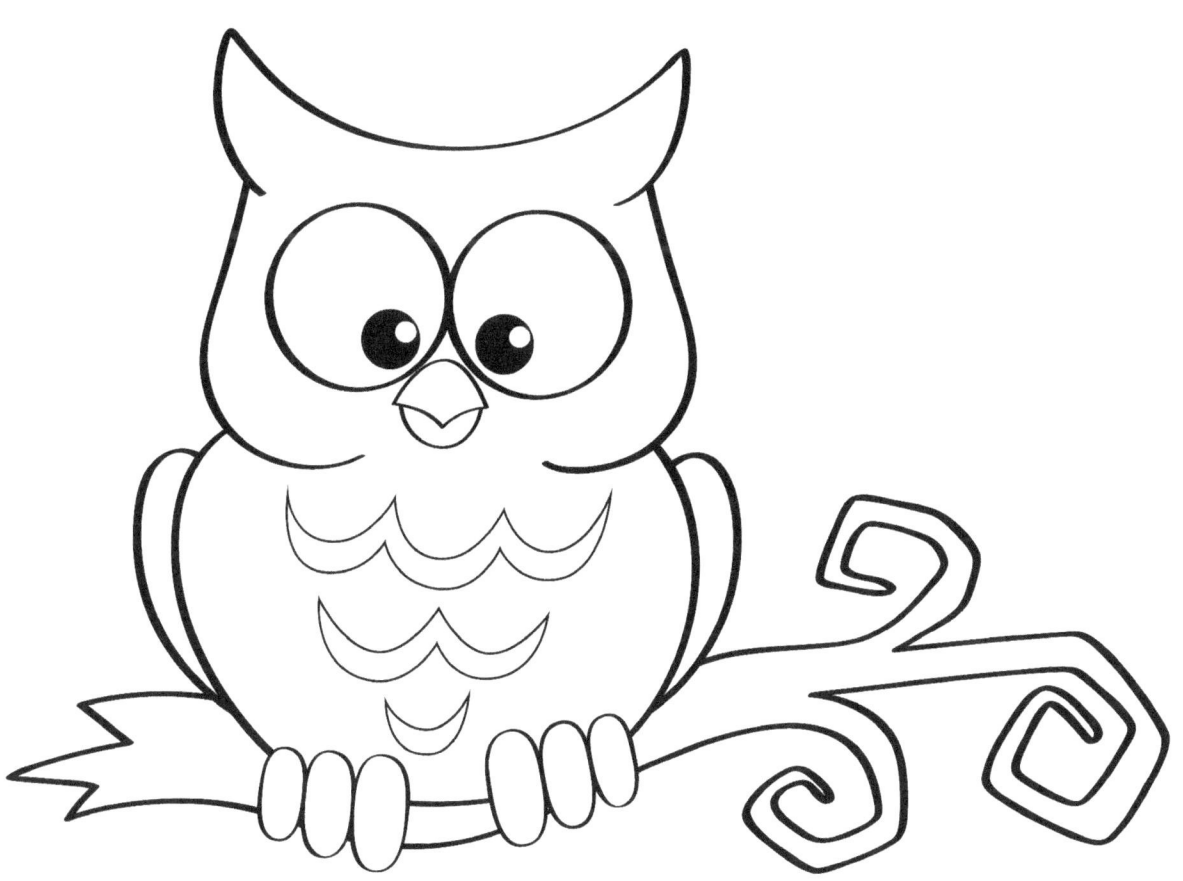

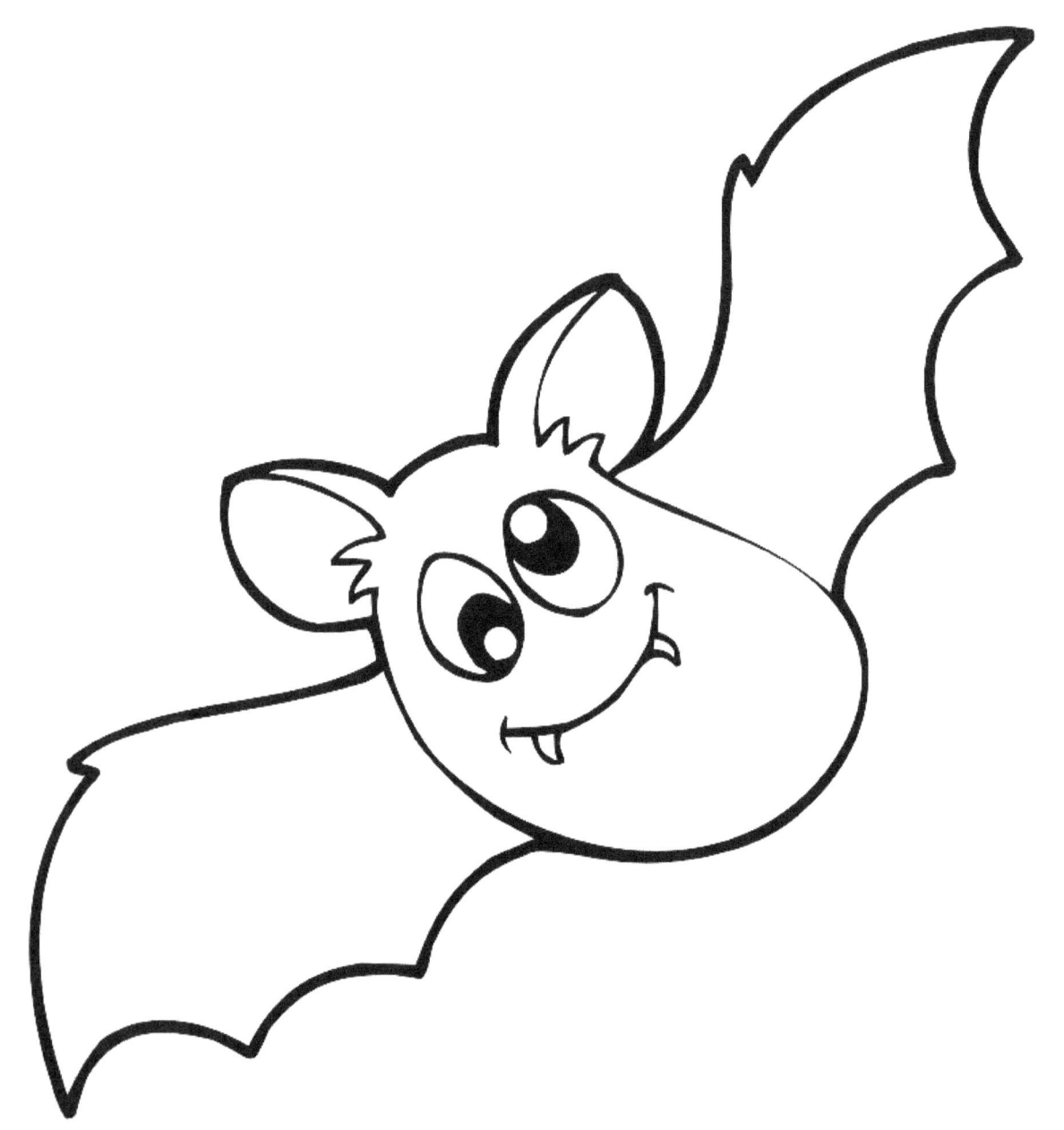

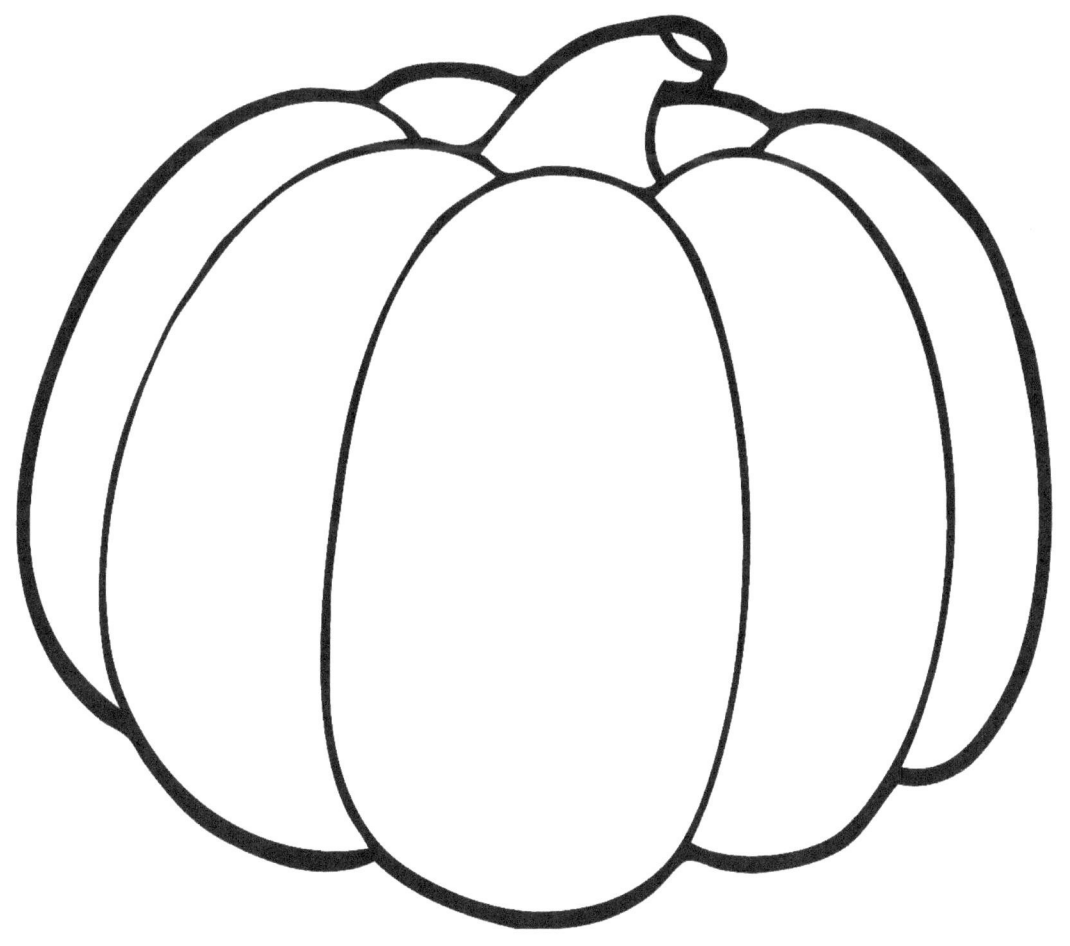

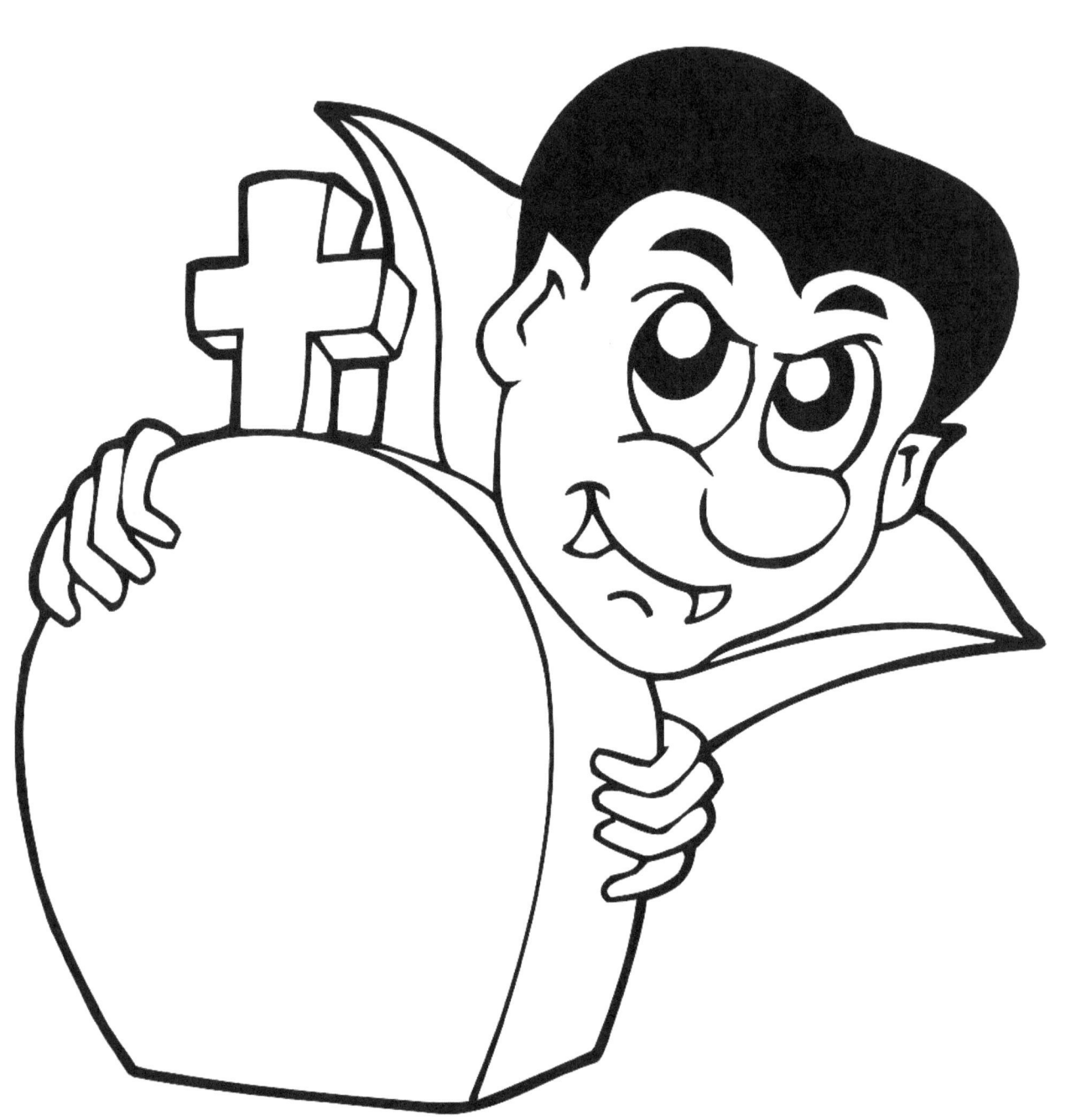

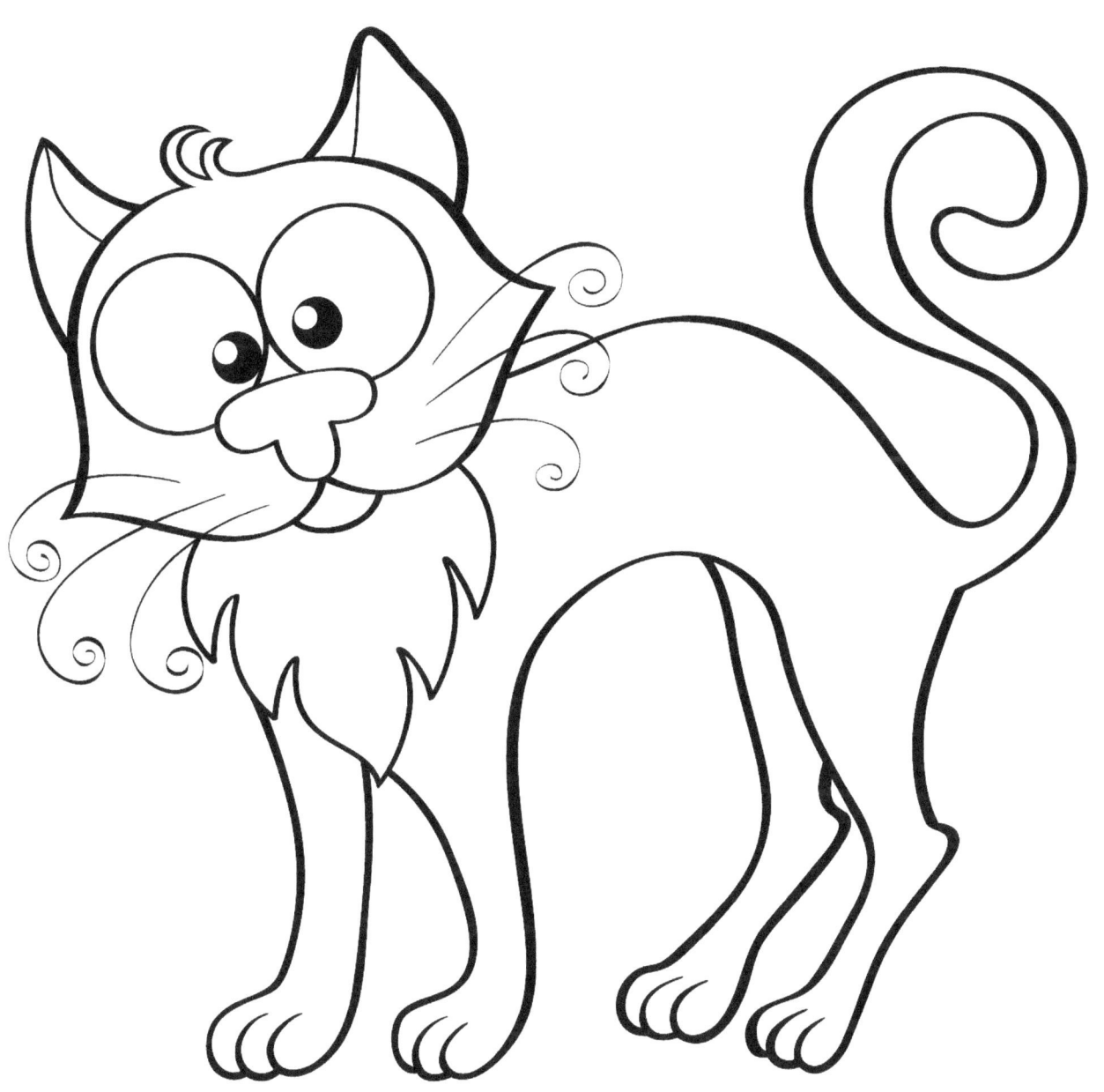

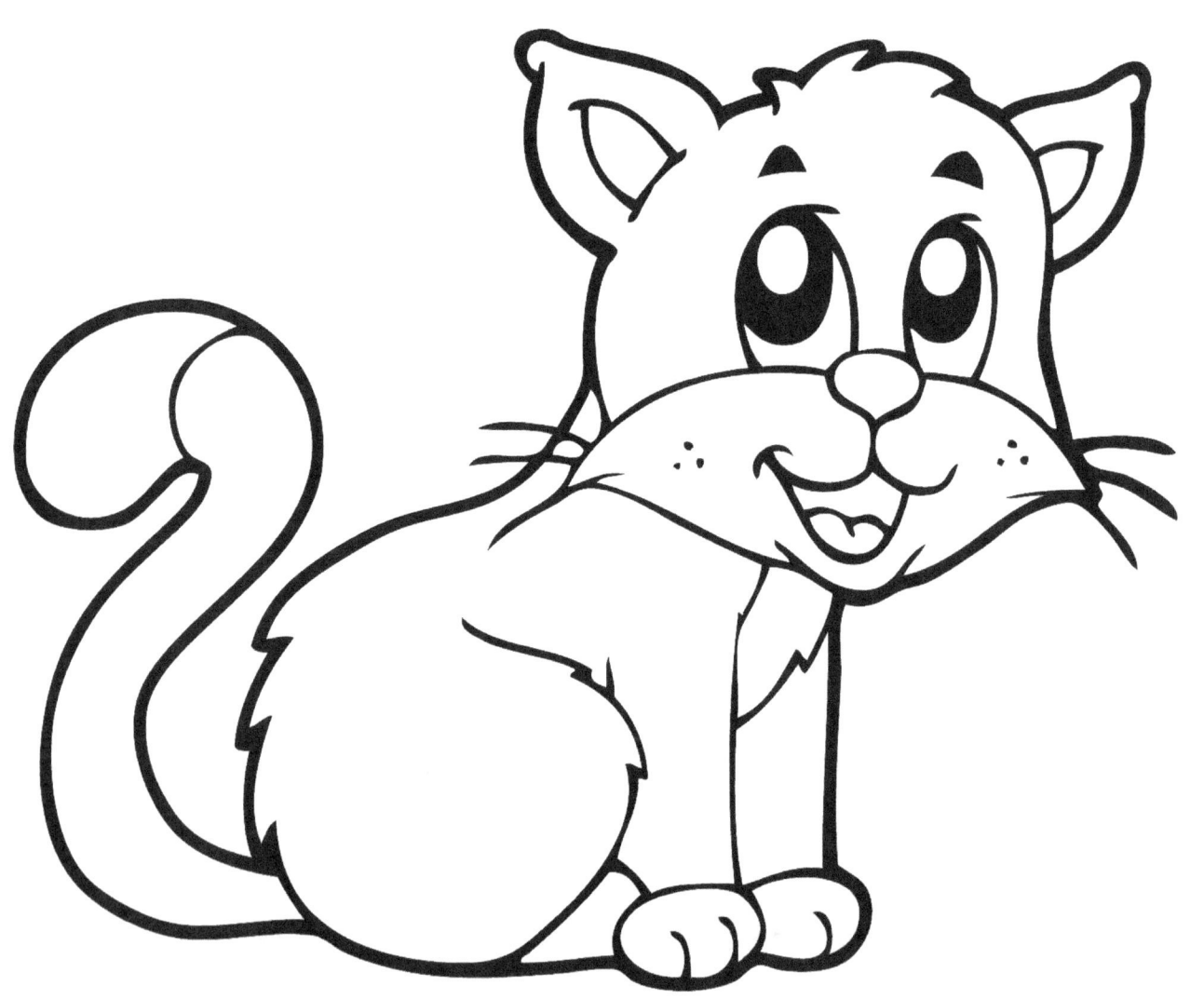

HALLOWEEN
Bingo

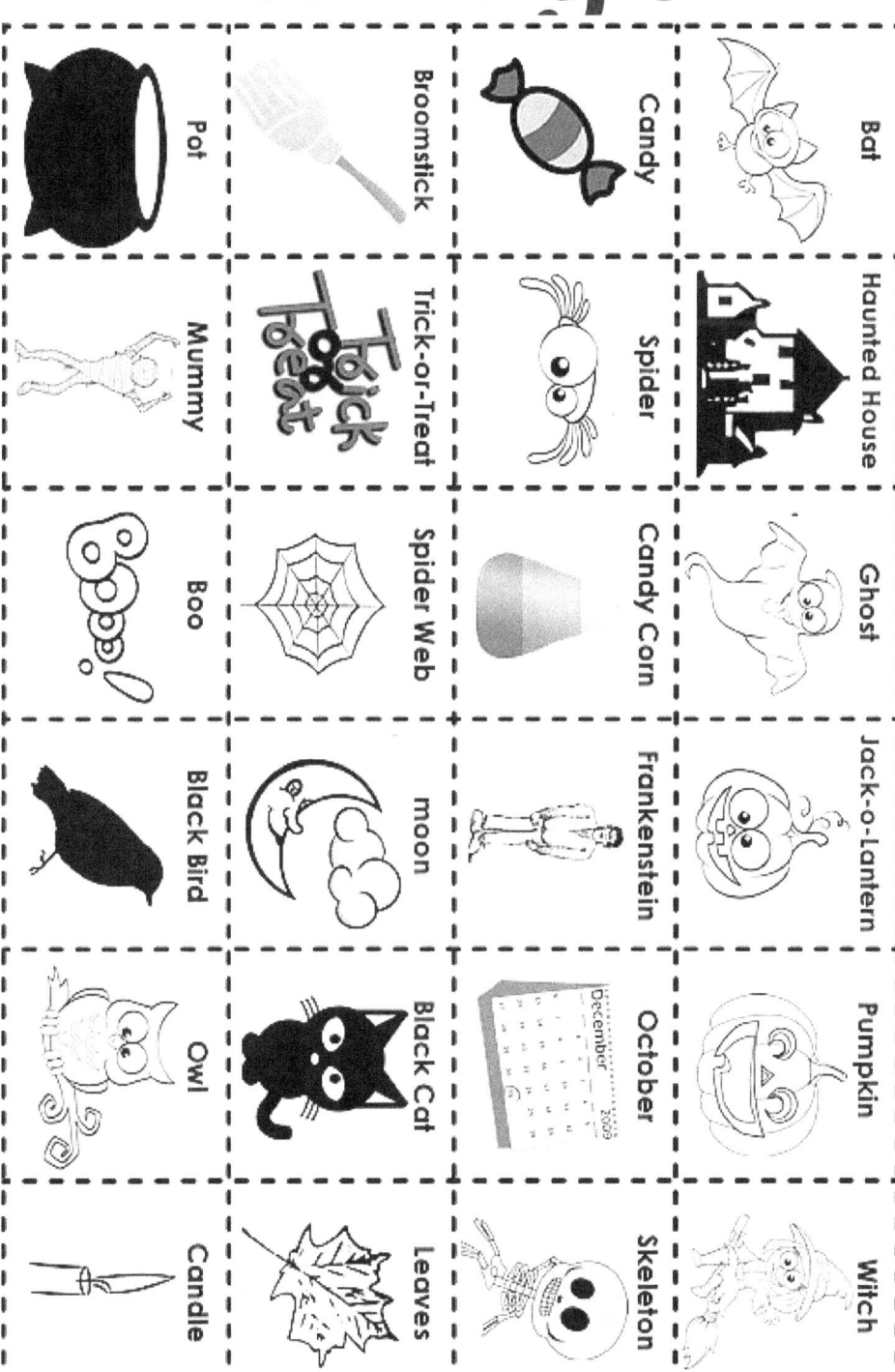

Pot	Broomstick	Candy	Bat
Mummy	Trick-or-Treat	Spider	Haunted House
Boo	Spider Web	Candy Corn	Ghost
Black Bird	moon	Frankenstein	Jack-o-Lantern
Owl	Black Cat	October	Pumpkin
Candle	Leaves	Skeleton	Witch

HALLOWEEN
Bingo

		Free Space		

HALLOWEEN
Bingo

Materials:

- Halloween picture squares (one sheet per children, plus an extra copy to use as calling cards)
- scissors
- glue
- Cut out the Halloween picture squares.
- Glue them in random order on their bingo board.

Playing the game:

- The caller will randomly select Halloween words from a bowl.
- When an item is called, all players mark it on their bingo board.
- The first player to get five items in a straight line (horizontally, vertically, or diagonally) wins

Notes

- This game can be played with your whole class, or students can play in small groups.
  You may want to offer a small prize for the winners.

www.ingramcontent.com/pod-product-compliance
Lightning Source LLC
Chambersburg PA
CBHW082304200526
45168CB00018B/3409